The Polar Bears of
Barrow, Alaska
the U.S.'s Most Northern Community

By John Tidwell

The Polar Bears of Barrow, Alaska
the U.S.'s most northern community

Library of Congress Control Number: 2011942226

ISBN: 978-1-57833-550-3

First Printing November, 2011

Printed by Everbest Printing Co. Ltd. in Guangzhou, China through **Alaska Print Brokers,** Anchorage, Alaska.

Book design: Vered R. Mares, 𝕿𝖔𝖉𝖉 𝕮𝖔𝖒𝖒𝖚𝖓𝖎𝖈𝖆𝖙𝖎𝖔𝖓𝖘
This book was typeset in 12 point Arno Pro.

Published by
Honest John's
Polar Bear Publishing Co.

Distributed by
𝕿𝖔𝖉𝖉 𝕮𝖔𝖒𝖒𝖚𝖓𝖎𝖈𝖆𝖙𝖎𝖔𝖓𝖘
611 E. 12th Ave.
Anchorage, Alaska 99501-4603
(907) 274-8633 (TODD) • Fax: (907) 929-5550
with other offices in Ketchikan, Juneau & Fairbanks, Alaska
sales@toddcom.com • **WWW.ALASKABOOKSANDCALENDARS.COM**

I have been enjoying the North Slope of Alaska since 1980, at first working for a private contractor and then with the local government. I loved the job and they paid me way more than I was worth. I, as they say, had it made. Then the plane crashed and after three years of rehabilitation I found that working eight hours a day was not in the cards. One would think that was the end of my world. Nay, nay, I had my ace in the hole, my hobby, photography. I am in no way a writer, so, thanks to my daughter's skill as an editor, you now have this collection of photos.

Before you get started I'll answer a few questions that just about everyone asks:

Have you ever been chased?

Many times, but never intentionally. Stalked too, sometimes intentionally to get a shot, but that is another story…

Do you carry a gun?

No! There are a couple of reasons for this. One is that you can't shoot a gun and a camera at the same time. Another reason is that usually someone is riding with me and they wouldn't want me to carry a gun because of my "reasoning". The "reason" is that there is a several thousand dollar fine and time in jail for shooting a bear. My "reasoning" is that I'd be better off shooting the person next to me to keep the bear busy while I made good my escape. The bear would eat the evidence, I'd be alive, no fine, and no jail time.

Would you want me to have a gun thinking the way I do?

Also remember we are in the bear's home uninvited. What right do I have to shoot a bear for being a bear? I get real upset when someone makes a movie and they have some guy with a gun standing behind them. If the bear acts like a bear he's dead. Is that fair?

Then there is the standard. What is the closest call you've ever had?

The one that almost got me had nothing to do with photography. I was using my son's pickup to go to the local landfill on a dark winter's night. (This was in the days when whale meat from the fall hunt was placed at the landfill inside city limits.) We all knew that bears came and went from the area but I didn't see any when backing in. Besides, sometimes you are so used to something you kind of look,

but not really. Well, I backed up to a pile of rubbish, stepped out, and reached in the back to grab a trash container. As I turned to throw it, twin cubs came around a pile of trash at the back of the truck. Not so bad, but momma then stuck her head around the pile. Luckily the truck door was open with the motor running. I turned, took one step, and hit the gear shift without even sitting up. Away I went. Once outside the gates I stopped the truck and lost my last meal.

Haven't changed my style much from those days but then that is another story…

I was out after a black guillemot picture mainly because there was so much in the news about them. It seems that this scientist had been studying them for more than 15 summers. Finally someone from a big magazine came out to get his story. The New York Times devoted a full section to his studies of the birds. Several of the locals used to take him supplies and help him set up out on an island. He ended up even getting on the Tonight Show. According to his tale, the biggest detriment to survival of the black guillemot was the polar bear.

Polar bears love eggs. Since he had all these nests for the birds, bears had a ready supply of eggs without having to search. They only had to open the boxes and reach in, kind of like us checking the chicken house. What we have in this picture are two birds swimming in an ice melt pond. The bottom of the pond is solid ice so they can't dive to the bottom, only paddle around. The bear however, is watching a seal hole that does allow access to the bottom. The female polar bear can dive through the hole but probably wouldn't need to. She is waiting for a seal to pop up through its breathing hole.

The picture was taken in June and the breathing hole is about two yards away. With a 300mm lens and using my van for a blind, I lay next to the front left tire with the camera in the continuous shooting mode. My coat wrapped around a bunch of pea gravel served as a steady mount. This is one of a series of shots taken at that time.

If I had been thinking I would have realized the shot would have been better off a tripod. I had considered a tripod, but I didn't want the bear to know I was out of the van. When a bear is this intense about a seal hole, there isn't much danger of it jumping up and coming after something as big as a van. But I wouldn't want to find out either.

Note the color of the ice. All ice is clear. It is the size and shape of the ice crystal that causes color. The deeper the color of the ice, the fresher and older the ice. Fresh water freezes and forces most of the salt out of the ice. Thus it is the oldest ice. If you were to taste the colored ice it would taste like fresh water.

There are two reasons for this. First it is old ice, thus it froze first because it has very little salt in it. Second, it is so cold it freezes taste buds and you can't taste any salt that may be present. To prove this all you do is take a taste of the icicle before it melts and then a taste of the water as it warms and starts to drip. If you were to crash out on the ice this would be the ice to look for so you wouldn't dehydrate. Of course, drinking fresh water would prevent damage to your organs, but would not restore your broken arms and legs.

A pair of black guillemots; a bear ready to pounce

For a long time my idea had been to catch a bear walking into the surf with footprints in the black sand. I got the idea a few years ago when boating through the channel between Plover Point and Crescent Island east of Barrow. We had taken the boat out to photograph bears from a water-to-land view, rather than land to water. Some ladies from California were with me and they had taken some great shots. One was a bear swimming at the top of a wave looking down at us when we were in the trough between waves. I can only imagine the stories told over that adventure.

I discovered at that point I couldn't control the boat and photograph at the same time. Therefore when seeing a bear in the surf on the return trip; I needed to forego the shot. Try as I might they failed to understand the shot, and rather than take it they preferred to chum the ocean with what was once breakfast. At this point it became clear that I shouldn't take people out who weren't willing to drive the boat. Lesson was learned, but the shot was still waiting in the wings.

A bear's paw prints leading to the shore edge; a bear stands in the water

Then along came this image. A beautiful, crisp October morning; no ice in sight and trying to get the ultimate King eider shot put me in the right spot. The eiders were swimming in Elson Lagoon and I wasn't paying a whole lot of attention to the Chukchi Sea side of the point.

A quick scan of the waterfowl of the Chukchi, done out of a habit, revealed a strange duck amongst the Bonaparte gulls. Low and behold, a metamorphosis took place; the duck became a bear. From his low angle he couldn't see me, which then made it my favorite game; wait and see what developed.

In October usually there is no ice around, making a landscape difficult. Quickly going through my wish list for shots, I remembered the bear in the surf shot. The bear in the surf part is easy, those footprints are what I was after. I am still missing the envisioned shot of huge surf, bear, and print shots from the water angle. With the right volunteer to drive the boat it will happen, I just don't know when. Until then, this ain't a bad substitute.

At the beginning of October, the sea ice is still a long way off. Then, how did I get pictures of bears on ice? No, contrary to what I wish some would say, there was no walking on water involved. Remember salt water freezes at a much colder temperature than fresh. Actually salt water doesn't freeze but the salt is forced out, then that residue freezes but that whole thing takes some explaining.

Sufficient to say, yes, there is some salt in sea ice but the sea itself is too salty to solidify. Back to how the picture came about. It was surprisingly enough not by accident.

We've had more bears around this summer and fall than normal. Thus an early start put me out on the tundra before daylight, moving in stealth mode to a set up alongside a fresh water pond next to the ocean.

Locals had cleaned out an ice cellar, so food was plentiful. Then all it took was patience to wait for a bear. One bear came from the town area and the other was already sleeping here before I arrived. Once they met, it was touch and go at first. Then these bears eventually made friends, as they are about the same size and age. They are not fighting but rather just playing. Several of the next shots are of the same bears. Usually one with the same landscape is all that's available but these guys were playing around enough to warrant extras.

Two bears play together on the ice

Having returned to Barrow in mid-August, the problem was not so much lack of bears, but rather lack of texture. As always, the difficulty was finding something to feature foreground or background so that it wouldn't look like a zoo shot. Remember, dirt and a bear doesn't market well. Those are tourist shots. I am not knocking tourist shots – only making apparent that I have the opportunity to wait around for the "moment", whereas they usually don't.

Anyhow, following a few days of drizzle, I woke to strong winds and partial sunshine this morning. Knowing that this would equal surf action along the Beaufort Sea side of Elson Lagoon, I gathered the gear and started making plans. I left town with high hopes that at least one of the three males seen several days before would still be in close.

Going out, the idea was to concentrate on an area where half of a grey whale had washed up several days before. Half a whale generally means orcas have been at work, so if we got lucky, perhaps they'd join us. I traveled up the right side of the peninsula and kept glassing the target area. Unfortunately the whale and bears were both gone.

Now option one is to go back and attack the "honey do" list with vigor. Option two – continue cruising for alternate opportunities. Heading back, if not quickly, at least steadily, with all the intention in the world of attacking that list I paused briefly to glass the remains of last year's whale harvest. Lo and behold, what was curled up next to a mandible that had washed up in the surf, but this guy. I decided a 28 to 105 mm lens with an F stop of 2.8 would give the best chance for a clean shot. My 400 has an F stop of 4.5 and with sun coming and going, I didn't want to take the chance of a cloud

Two bears tunnel in the ice with a gull overhead

coming over. The only thing left to do is wait for him to strike a pose, shoot as quickly as possible, pick the best and hope all ends well. Funny how sitting outside a store waiting for the wife, I get bored and irritable, but waiting for a bear to move just right doesn't bother me a bit. Yea! and I did forget about that list. But in my defense, look at this shot. Worth the procrastination?

A bear lies by a whale mandible; gulls flock overhead

Friday morning as I was working out at the local gymnasium, an announcement came over our radio station: "Attention! Be careful. There are four bears on the beach between town and NARL (Naval Arctic Research Laboratory.)" Naturally this requires a shortened work out. I jumped in the Suzuki, stopped at the house, grabbed cameras and be careful be darned. Unfortunately, all I got after that buildup was some mediocre photos, according to my wife. She said they didn't make the cut. We high grade photos and print out the ones a committee of friends grade every fall. Those are test marketed at the annual craft fair on the first Saturday in December. But then that is another story.

As I said, Friday didn't work out, but today is Monday and my niece (BAIT) has the day off and agrees to go out with me. She had never seen a bear, let alone a polar bear in the wild. Usually Mondays aren't that great a day as bears have been bothered all weekend by snow machines running around. Tuesday through Saturday morning is best for bears, as that is when most people are at work. Bears have had all Monday to calm down. That being said, as many details as possible that make for a successful shoot are addressed. Full tank of fuel, radiator fluid, fresh camera batteries, in position before first light, lower tire pressure, that's all you need to know. Didn't think I'd tell you everything did you?

When we first arrived, you could barely see the quarter mile to where the bears could be feeding. Fog and twilight kind of put a sheer curtain over the whole scene. Night vision binoculars reveal there are bears. As I lowered the tire pressure before going off road, I told BAIT to watch the bears. A snowmachine had passed by and the bears had run into the ocean. The hope was that the bears would return or swim along the coast and we'd get some shots anyway, just in a different location. If she watched, then it wouldn't be so hard to spot them again. Getting back in the Suzuki, ready to go, I casually asked if bears were back. Being the trusting soul that I am, though, she said no, I checked to be sure. Obviously they were back or this picture wouldn't be here. Anyhow, we did end up getting some decent stuff but nothing that didn't include old whale bones which aren't exactly picturesque. Within a short time they started to move up the coast and away from the bones. Since BAIT had risked my hide by saying the bears weren't back, I thought it only fair that she attract their attention. My thought was she could get out of the Suzuki and make dying seal sounds and it would do the trick. Bears would come back to investigate and the shots would be great. After all I would be perfectly safe in the Suzuki and if it got dangerous I'd try and warn her. Since she didn't appreciate my sense of adventure, we had to settle for what you see here. I love those pastel skies and the ocean when it turns to Jell-O. Unfortunately, to get the bears in focus, a sacrifice has to be made on the Jell-O textured ocean and sky colors. Someday I am going to learn how to get all that good stuff in.

Three bears feed at the shoreline

A mother bear scouts the area while a cub waits by her side

Knowing bears were out and about at Point Barrow I was anxious to see if there was a chance to get a decent closeup. However, there were things that should be accomplished around the house. During a brief moment of procrastination, before I enthusiastically attacked the "honey do" list, a tour bus arrived to look at our dog team. While discussing dogs I mentioned that I really wanted to go out to the Point to see some bears I knew would be there. A lady in the group volunteered to pay for gas if I would take her. I had after all, "guaranteed" bears. Normally I don't go out on a limb and say there are definitely going to be bears, but this day was special. Bears had been in the same area for two weeks, and earlier in the day I had seen them with my binoculars from a few miles away. You might think this would be next to impossible, but remember we don't have trees to clutter up the view.

It is not uncommon to sit on the beach and watch bears hunt whenever the ice pack is close in. After a brief struggle with my dilemma between "The List" or photographing bears, off we went. She commented to me on the way out that having come from Norway and being this close to the furthest point north in America she might as well go all the way. With the promise of a polar bear at the end of the trail she wasn't going to pass up the opportunity. Obviously, when she rejoined the group with a picture and a certificate of an official polar bear sighting, they were wishing they had gone too.

This mother and cub had been coming in for whale scraps for a couple of days. She would wait until males and or larger mothers and their cubs had fed, then come in for her turn. The reason for standing up is to get a better view and figure out if there is any danger around for her cub. Bears are creatures of habit. Thus, it was usual to see her about mid-day coming out of the ice field. After watching for a few days, finding a good spot to intercept her was the only problem to overcome. We were lucky and hit the right spot at the right time. She didn't see my approach and it worked out great. Even though bears get used to vehicles sitting in a particular area it generally makes them skittish if it is moving. Sitting still and waiting is the best way I've found to photograph bears. This mother isn't a particularly nervous mother, but no bear likes to be surprised. Once she recognized the vehicle as non-threatening, it was business as usual. You may see other pictures I've taken with her as the subject, and begin to recognize her. She passes on a birthmark to each cub and that is how I know it is her or one of her offspring. As far as getting pictures of bears she is one of the easiest to get shots of, as long as you are respectful of her space and sit quietly.

These are black guillemots and a male polar bear. As you've probably figured out by looking at other shots, I like these little birds. The image of birds reflected in the pool is meant to draw your eye in, and then catch the bear in the background. I got the idea from reading an ad for a camera. It shows a rock wall and some trees – then you notice a wolf. Because a picture of a bear is just a picture of a bear, no one ever knows if it was taken at a zoo or not. To set your picture apart from everyone else's a lot of time is spent on finding interesting backgrounds. When we go out I try and set some kind of goal for a shot. Ideas are gleaned from magazines and people that ride with me. Some want multiple animals and others may want ice formations. The birder that was with me really didn't care if we got a bear or not.

What we did want is some red phalarope or black guillemots, in an ice melt pond, preferably. Others he was interested in were snowy owl, jaegers and loons. The idea was to collect enough photos from his trip to make a family calendar. Since he was a birder, Barrow was a natural choice.

We took off at 8 p.m. following check-in at the King Eider hotel. From discussions before arrival came a list of birds. After thinking about the shoot, I decided we'd go for eiders, snowy owl and jaegers out by fresh water lake. We lucked out and got white fronted geese and tundra swans as a bonus. A kind of mixed blessing was an Arctic fox. He was such a distraction for the birds that it helped us get some close-ups. Unfortunately he did get some eggs. A snowy rolled him a few times and that ended that. This shot was taken off the dirt berm opposite the boat launch at the other end of town. It was close to midnight with very little traffic when we shot these and that accounts for the bear being in so close. This male was big enough to hold his own at the Point and probably was just wandering around from boredom. We were successful on this shoot because there was enough lead time to have pre-scouted our shoot sites. The reflection and the bear were pure accident.

A male bear passes by a group of black guillemots

This picture came about due to a request for pictures of icebergs from my wife. She wanted to put together a collage of Arctic scenes and didn't want it to be all bears. In the spirit of cooperation I went to see what I could see. July usually has some larger bergs still hanging around even though the ice pack itself has gone out, so it wasn't a big deal. If this was in August, it probably would have been necessary to use the boat, but it could still be done. About the only time icebergs are difficult to photograph is September through October. Personally I don't like photographing off the boat. Everybody else is shooting while I maneuver the boat. Once in awhile I get someone who'll drive, then it's fun. Notice the ice shelf in the background? That's where you'd expect to find a bear. They like to lie on, or float along next to a shelf such as this because seals can easily get on them. When floating alongside scoping out the berg they just dog paddle with barely a ripple. A bear can then attack any number of ways.

From the top they stalk, or they swim alongside and go up and over the side. My particular favorite is from under the ice. They spot a seal, dive underneath, and come up through the soft ice before the seal even knows what's happening. Therefore the berg in this picture shouldn't have bears around it as there isn't anything to draw them in. We checked out the beach after the bear left and there was no forage in the area. I learn more about these bears every day, and what I have come to know for sure, is that I know nothing for sure. Anyway, at first we didn't see the bear because it was swimming in the pool and we assumed it was just a duck or gull splashing around. We were admiring the ice formation and checking out the different angles for a picture when out pops a head. The minute she was visible it was all hands on deck. Luckily the cameras were already out and this is actually one of the first pictures taken.

Everyone had set their cameras for continuous shooting, so each time she became visible all you could hear was the music of power drives. Of course, as always, we end up with a ton of pictures of the back of the head, and this and that body part shots. I am sure you all have shots that aren't quite what you were after, but close.

That is one of the best features of digital, all those almost shots can be dumped. No more box full of pictures and loose negatives

that came from "what envelope"? Now all you have to remember is where you stored the CD. I used a 300mm lens and a window mount stabilizer, so most of the shots were clear. Taking pictures like this so close to the edge of the water, the sand and pea gravel makes me nervous. I am always considering the "what ifs". What if I get stuck in the sand or worse yet, the vehicle slides into the water. So many things can happen to ruin your day. It's not like you are in a wildlife park or zoo and you have control over the animals. All said and done, this was one of my favorite shots and a great day.

A female bear emerges from underneath an iceberg

In the early 1980's I came to Barrow, Alaska for a six week job managing a plumbing shop. While on assignment in Anaktuvuk Pass, the beauty was such that I was inspired to get serious about photography. Following a plane crash in 1996, I retired and now enjoy photography full time. The polar bear picture you are looking at was taken in Barrow. Polar bears may be found here almost any time during the year, especially if the ice pack is close. Naturally some months are better than others. An example of this was when 150 bears stayed for the summer. But then that's another story.

How did I get this picture? These bears were sleeping about 100 yards off shore. The ice they were on was one of the few areas that were solid, but not solid enough to hold a human. It was early October and I hadn't expected to see any ice of substance yet. This gift of the floe was much appreciated as I had been going through a long dry spell without bears. The wind and current had brought in the floe. Remember we don't have tides here, only wind and current changes sea action. Scientists say it's because we are too far north for the moon to affect the sea height. If we do have a

Two bears walk the ice on a floe

tide it would only be four inches or so. I had expected to see seal on the open water.

From the city of Barrow to Point Barrow there had been no ice. As I topped the small ridge at the end of land, which is the farthest point north in the U.S., it was a pleasant surprise. All week long I had wondered why there were tracks on the beach every other day or so but never did see a bear. Now it made sense. The floe had been over the horizon and they had been swimming in occasionally to dine on beach carrion. Anyhow in the distance I could see some single bears in different locations, but on the same floe. As they were single they were more than likely males. The choice was to try and sneak up on the sleeping bears or wait to see if one or more singles came in and get some interaction shots.

As a bird in the hand is better than a hope, I opted for the sleeping pair. I moved into position as quietly as possible. Of course sitting there all kind of scenarios ran through my mind. Somebody might come in a boat; a plane could swing in low or a chopper with a scientist swoop in for a look. Luckily before any of the negative stuff interfered (in less than an hour) they noticed my vehicle and got inquisitive. This is one of many shots as they came in for a better look. I count on bears being inquisitive for a lot of shots. A trick to use sometimes is to hang a piece of cloth from a stick that can be seen for a considerable distance. For some reason bears, especially young ones, can't resist checking it out. I've had bears come in from a mile out and investigate the rag blowing in the wind before going for food that's plentiful. On this shot you may wonder at what point I chickened out and left. Mama got to within about 50 feet and stood up, satisfied her curiosity, turned around and went back out on the ice. If they had come much closer my tail lights would have been all they'd have remembered. Generally if I just stay still and quiet, bears will look me over and leave as I am just an inanimate object and not a threat. Remember I did say, GENERALLY.

A small megapixel camera is better than no camera. I had failed to charge the battery on the good cameras sufficient to last a whole day of shooting. Ah! But, I did have a back up just in case. We had been out since early afternoon even though it was a foggy day. Actually I prefer bad weather as most people stay in town and the beach is mine. True, pictures aren't bright and sunny, but then that's not real life is it?

Anyhow it was about 7 p.m. with rain adding to the mix when we caught this female and her cubs moving on the floe. Luckily I had an umbrella so we set up tripods on the beach. The umbrella keeps rain off the camera lens and is a must unless you have a sunshade for your lens.

The situation was the male was sleeping and she just walked right in on him. He really jumped when she showed up. Usually mothers with babies, or even another male, would shy away from a guy this size. The body language shows you they were warning him not to start anything. Because of the size of her young, she wasn't worried about him killing her young, and let's face it, they outnumbered him. I still can't figure out why she didn't go around him. The confrontation didn't need to happen. But then I don't think like a bear and they probably don't think like me. If they did think like us I am sure they'd have got me by now. I don't usually print 8" x 10" prints off a 2 mega-pixel camera, but my wife insisted, and that is why you have a copy.

A female bear and her two cubs walk past a startled male bear

One of the frustrations of wildlife photography is sitting for hours and then just before the subject is in the right spot something happens that changes everything. That is why one of the best times to photograph is in the middle of the night. With 24 hours of daylight the general population is home snug in bed and the world is ours. Visitors to Barrow that buy into to this logic have an excellent chance to see bears close up in the spring and summer months. We can go out about 11 in the evening and stay for several hours without the concern of catching a plane, or being interrupted by someone on a 4–wheeler or whatever. Nobody has ever complained to me about losing sleep when they've got themselves a good bear picture. The picture you are looking at was taken during the first week in August about 3 a.m.

As I have said before, August isn't usually that great for ice close in, but there had been some stiff winds which blew this berg in. It is grounded up against the beach and was only here for a day. If you look closely you'll notice the thin ice sheets in the background. Big sheets of ice for seal habitat, usually equals bears in an area. This information is what convinced the visitors to go out with me and they were justly rewarded for the loss of sleep. Actually what I told them is that we'd probably end up with zoom lens shots of bears as they floated by on the ice. This one with the bear walking down the beach was a surprise to me. I've not had a lot of luck marketing this one, but that's probably because people don't recognize the significance of where it is. This picture was taken at Point Barrow, the farthest point north in the U.S. The hill behind the bear is the site of an ancient village

several hundred years old. After a storm artifacts are usually found right on the beach. Even today a stone spear head occasionally is uncovered by wind and waves. If you are in Barrow, check out the local museum and science center to view what's been found. When we're out and find something of historical importance, it's to be left alone and reported to the science center. Unless something is in danger of being lost to the elements, then we're to write down the particulars of the area and turn it in for all to enjoy. Your name is placed on the item in recognition of your contribution.

A bear walks down the beach

This is a November picture. It is just as cold as it looks. Even though the temperature was at least 15 above, the wind really makes a difference. Besides fall being beautiful, it's usually best for quantity of bears. Light is the biggest challenge to deal with. Towards the end of January, when the sun starts to come back, we get great color and bears, but by then the cold is almost too much for most. But with the sun up all at once it makes the winter go quickly.

This is basically a display picture to show people when they want to go out with me what they should expect to see. My wife said I should print it out so they wouldn't waste their time if they decided to go out with me. Some won't be happy for a shot in the dark. The image has been lightened up some on the computer. Nowadays you can take your film into a film processor and get a CD back. Then go in and adjust contrast, darken or lighten and whatever else you want to play with.

This picture was taken while demonstrating the benefits of just sitting still and letting the bear come to you. One would think you could see a bear, then speed your vehicle up and get a picture before it gets away. First, a bear can out accelerate most vehicles you can think of. Then there is the matter of getting a picture in a hurry. The third problem is you are harassing bears by making them run from you. To sum it up you are not going to get decent bear pictures by harassing them. I have found that being in the right place at the right time is the best way. It's just a simple matter of monitoring them daily. In this case we were getting close ups when the bear heard a snowmachine coming and decided to head for the ice. I took the picture because the moon fit in the lens. Without the moon it would just be another bear picture.

A bear walks in the view of the November moon

A bear leaves town, heading to Point Barrow for scraps

I cheated on this photo. Sitting up listening to my scanner is a lot easier than driving around in the snow up and down the beach. The morning radio traffic was the usual stuff when everyone is taking off for work. That's when I heard the magic word "bear". Listening closer it seemed it was around the beach area near the cleaners. Now that would probably mean that Public Safety would chase it out onto the sea ice if possible, then try and get it to go north. Bears usually are chased towards the north of town so they'll find the food source out towards Point Barrow.

Following the fall whale hunt, the town is cleaned up and whale bones or scraps are set out at Point Barrow so that bears have less reason to come into town. Doing this also cuts down on the number of foxes hanging around. Fox all have the rabies gene but they don't all have active rabies. Rabies is generally brought about by starvation, so it's best to keep them out of town. Bears make big pieces into little pieces and fox appreciate the help. If this bear chose to go south then it would probably just come back later in the day. My idea was to get ahead of the bear and get a photo with town in the background if possible. A quick decision on what vehicle to take was imperative. I must confess I chose a snowmachine. Snowmachines are notorious for not starting at the most inconvenient times, but obviously this wasn't one of them. If I used my Suzuki then I'd have a problem if it was already out on the ice when I got there. On the other hand, if it headed south there would be enough time to go home, get the Suzuki and follow along or better yet set up in the line of travel. As this shot was going to be under flat light conditions the position of the light source would not figure into the equation.

It would have been preferable to have more of the town in the background, but there were some unforeseen problems. For one thing I was so hyped up the camera was set on manual focus not automatic. I also fell down getting off the machine. Try and wipe off the lens and check to find why the camera won't focus when a bear is coming at you. Then add to the mix that a decision needs to be made whether to turn the engine off or not, so you don't spook the bear and can use the seat as a camera rest. As it turned out I got the shot and lived. Without a 400mm lens this picture would not have been made. The thought process was with a 400 mm there would be enough time to start the engine after a few quick shots and get out of the way. Fortunately there was a lens hood on the camera so the blowing snow didn't screw up the picture. Some would say that my thought process on what's safe and not so safe leaves room for improvement. But then there are those who would prefer to die without the assistance, or because of, an adrenaline rush. This was taken with a Canon 100 to 400mm lens, F stop of 4 to 5.6 with image stabilization on a Canon 10D.

April 2009 and spring is a month early. As a matter of fact for the last five years it has kept creeping up on an earlier start. At this point April weather is what May used to be. The ice pack hasn't opened up which has prevented whaling and the ice has started to rot. Taking this into consideration helps explain why bears are few and far between. With less people on the ice and seals easier to get they don't need to run the gauntlet to the whale bone pile.

That's why I appreciate the opportunity to shoot this guy so close to Barrow. My wife wanted to show our neighbor lady's daughter a bear before she left town. Trying to get a shot with a non-photographer is usually more dif-

Gulls fly past a bear

ficult because they usually don't have the patience to keep at it day after day. In this case it took three trips out to finally score a shot. About 9:30 in the evening we were driving down the beach when this one was spotted about a mile away. We dropped below the horizon and moved slowly towards our victim. Bear are used to the sound of machinery so the motor is just white noise to them. The main concern is to not have them see you moving, especially not moving fast. OK! We are about 100 yards out and just below a slight rise. Once we come out of this depression there is nowhere to hide.

The hope is that he doesn't glance our way as we move in for the shot. In order to avoid turning sideways we'll need to shoot from outside the vehicle. Turning sideways is saying "see how big I am, move away – the food source is mine". Being lucky is sometimes better than good, as he does look our way yet doesn't take off. The creeping along a few inches at a time really paid off. Time to get out and shoot, keeping the Hummer directly behind us, and of course close. It only took about fifty shots, but each one was clear so the only problem then was to pick out the one that would market. The reason for the high amount of printable shots has to be credited to a good tripod.

Shooting with a good base usually accounts for a high percentage of marketable shots as far as clarity goes. Shooting free hand is a crap shoot, you just don't know. The best advice I ever received was to use a tripod, monopod, bean bag, or anything else available but

free hand only as last resort. The handiest monopod around is the dual purpose short square handled shovel. Stick it in the sand and you're good to shoot, or dig out of a hole. But then that is another story.

Generally shooting in early fall isn't a preference, but, seeing how the grasses were now in color it increased the chances of a marketable shot. I had been out at Point Barrow, attempting to get a female and cub with this vibrantly colored landscape. Obviously it didn't work out as planned and therefore this shot you are looking at is a result of plan "B".

As related before "the only bad camera" is the one you don't have when an opportunity presents itself. I point this out because of the following opportunity. The short eared owl in this photo was sitting

A bear moves over the snow, hunting

on a trash can farming the drainage ditch as I pulled into my driveway. True owl photos don't market well, but what the heck, this is only a game anyway.

A short-eared owl is not the best subject, but we did have that great color in the landscape. The challenge of getting a shot that would combine basic owl coloring and those grasses seemed like a good game for the day. Try as I might I just couldn't get that killer shot, or at least what I thought might be a killer shot. I ended up shooting this guy with lemmings and all those great floral colors. Nothing seemed to work up to what I wanted. Then this "photo op" came. I was lying on the deck shooting this guy in different situations when he landed on the other side of the house.

A short-eared owl hunts for lemmings in tall grass

To get this shot I had to remain as motionless as possible. So motionless, snowbirds actually landed on me while waiting for the moment. Back to the statement "no bad camera except the one you don't have". When shooting wildlife in motion, a fast camera is better. Also knowing when a subject is going to move isn't a bad thing either.

This is what I consider just about close enough. I was talking to this guy in Fairbanks that really wanted to see a bear up close. He's a friend of my son and had a free ticket for taking a bump on a flight a year ago. While they were discussing the Arctic, my son volunteered to have me take him out. He called and I suggested Wednesday – first plane in, and leave the following morning or evening. By coming in on the morning flight, we go out as soon as he touches down. Then in the evening we've got all night long, if that's what it took to get the picture. If no luck, we'd still have all Thursday. If you have this much time and bears are in the area, it's about 90% chance of getting the photo. Frustration was the name of the game at first as the bears were around but so far out all we could get was a spot in the picture. Me and my big mouth about getting in close was the main problem. He had brought a camera with a 50mm lens with no zoom, because I said "no problem". With a 300mm I would have looked like a genius but as it was, I was at the opposite end of the spectrum.

We were able to see several bears but nothing to write home about. I figured that if we hadn't got anything by 2 p.m. there were just too many people around for a bear to come in close, so we gave up until evening. Out by 10 p.m. and ready to go – so we brought a lunch. Good thing we did because it wasn't until about 1 a.m. that we came up with this shot. When we first got out to the area, there were just too many people around. Campfires and 4 wheelers were spaced so that a bear would think he was running a gauntlet if he had come to shore.

What we did until the population cleared out and went home is go birding. I love to shoot pictures of birds so this wasn't a bad thing as far as I was concerned. We have loons and eiders in breeding colors along with several other species and some people come here just for the birds.

Anyway, after everyone left, we parked up a little draw on the beach and watched the ice. Sure enough, about an hour after things calmed down, here comes a bear gliding along through the ice. He actually came on to shore about a quarter mile from us and we considered going down the beach and try to get around him. However, the decision was to sit and see what happened. As soon as he headed our way we just climbed back in the van and waited. That's always the hardest part of photography – "waiting". As you sit there and can't see your target, it's always second guessing time. Has the bear gone the other way? Is he back in the water? Has he got around us somehow? If I open the door and try to see where he's at, will he see me and take off? Will he be close and get me? Luckily he hadn't gone around. Noticing the speed and body language this one wasn't stopping until it got to us and maybe not then. As I said in the beginning, this is close enough. Time to start the engine and leave.

A bear walks up the beach

A female bear rests with her two cubs

I called this Smurf Village. Remember the cartoon Smurfs? Originally these mushroom type bergs were taller than they are in this photo. After a spring and summer of melting they eventually just collapsed but it was good for awhile. When these conditions show up it is the absolute best for looking for bears. Look for broken up ice, ponds of fresh water, seal habitat; it just doesn't get much better. You can sit and just keep glassing and you WILL see bears as long as there are no snowmachines out on the ice. Because of the broken up ice, the machines usually don't go out in this area. What I like to do is find a place where there isn't anyone else around and continue to glass the area until we come up with a bear. The object is to pick the most likely bear or bears to come in and get ahead of them so when they hit the beach we are set up and ready to go.

Now sometimes it takes hours of just watching bears do what bears do and a little luck but it can be so rewarding. This mother is a usual in the Barrow area. She and her offspring are easily recognized by the birthmark on her nose that she passes on to her cubs. Knowing your target and her hangouts helps when we are attempting this move.

We've spotted the bears, recognized them, and know the direction of travel. The hardest part of this trip was trying to keep focused.

When there are other bears around you start second guessing yourself – especially if another bear seems to be headed into another area, faster than the one you are aiming for.

Then the decision comes, do I dare move or do we stick to the original plan? Obviously we went for the twins. It was a little hairy for awhile as a male picked up the scent and followed along for awhile. You'll notice even with the twins, she isn't acting aggressive as close as we are. She is a dangerous bear because she doesn't seem to have a natural fear of man.

The picture was taken with a 70 to 210 lens and the van was full of people. When she first came to Barrow she had paint on her, so she must have been marked by Fish and Game. Not much else to tell you on this picture because she just sits on the beach and stares back at you, which doesn't make for much of a story. I have shots of her and her babies in several locations but this one with the ice in back is one of my favorites.

I call this picture 'lovers'. This is a male and female during breeding season. The size difference is typical as males are usually remarkably bigger than females. Because of their interest in each other, we were able to get fairly close. The gulls in the picture are a bonus. Actually the gulls are a major factor in getting pictures like this. In the spring if you see gulls flying around an area you can assume they are feeding. They are the trash technicians of the Arctic. Anyhow once we sight the gulls, it's just a simple matter of being alert, finding why they are feeding, then, moving in slowly. Arctic fox also follow bears around. If you can figure out where they are coming from, or going to, chances go way up for finding a bear.

What we've done here is cruise along the ice looking over fields of soft snow. We'd already seen the gulls, so as soon as we found fox track we headed off in the same direction; we were now headed out with purpose. Ice fields go for miles and the bergs are huge so we needed to pay attention. Stop, look, and listen is the name of the game. The ice is absolutely beautiful. We drive in and out of football stadium size areas where the color is so intense it hurts your eyes. Tracks from fox and bear going up and over drifts and bergs to who knows where. Sound travels a long way and a fox yipping is what we were listening for. Deep breathing or what sounds like deep breathing is what we hear, coming from the other side of the pressure ridge. So here is the set up. I hear what sounds like a bear breathing deep, possibly from running from me. But on the other hand it could be a whale using a breathing hole. Or! A whale breathing and a bear trying to figure out how to take him.

Bears have been known to take large pieces of ice and drop them on a whale's head to knock him out. Then they drag the whale onto the ice. Can I get to the other side and back out again if things go bad? The trail between the icebergs is enough to pass through but there is nowhere to turn the snowmachine around if I come face to face with a bear. Also vibration will ruin the shot if the machine is left running. For all these reasons we now have this particular shot. I just didn't have the nerve to go around the corner of the berg to see what was on the other side. We simply looked around for some bears that didn't pose much of a problem when it came to an escape route. The bergs are small and I have a large field of flat ice to take off across and a 400mm lens. This picture was shot off a tripod next to a snowmachine that was <u>not </u>shut off to prevent vibration. My kind of shot….reasonably safe.

Two bears during mating season; gulls flock beside them

Day after day tourists and locals were coming out to photograph the gathering of the bears. On this particular day there were 159 bears on the beach. The count comes from the 10 other people who all came out with the same number. Under normal conditions bears aren't known to share territory as it is hard enough for one bear to find enough to eat let alone several. Barrow is the exception to the norm. Whale bones in the background had been placed there following the October hunt pursuant to usual operating procedures. By placing the bones here bears have one less reason to come into town looking for food. Usually every spring and first part of summer it is possible to find one or two bears in the general area of the bones. They continue to hang around as long as the Arctic ice pack is in close. Even during August and September if you go out first thing in the morning or late in the evening you have a real good chance of finding one. If you do this remember to look for tracks and follow them.

Bears curl up against a wind break and they are hard to see if they don't move. Yes I know they are white or nearly so but they can look an awful lot like a piece of driftwood when next to a log. They also dig out holes in the sand and all you can see is a little bit of fur. Many times I've passed up bears as beach debris only to look back and see a bear watching me. My suggestion to those that call about coming to see bears is, try for Tuesday through Friday morning. Friday afternoon through Sunday there are just so many people around that it stresses them out and usually they'll go find a place to hide. Now I am not saying you can't find a bear or won't find any on the weekend but your chances increase during the week.

What caused this Woodstock for bears was that in July the ice blew out over night and bears in the Barrow area were left stranded. Usually the same amount of bears are around but scattered in a large area. Because they swim back and forth between land and ice to feed on the whale bones, you're not really aware of the numbers until something like this happens. This time the ice went out about 300 miles overnight, according to satellite photographs. So bears hung out for most of the summer.

I've only seen such a large concentration one other time, and there weren't near this many bears. That time there were 37 bears on a grey whale carcass about 20 miles south of town. The local airline shut down for the afternoon and took all their employees down for a look see. The grey whale they are feeding on in the foreground had washed up the day before. Every bear here is a polar bear. Some look like brown bears because they are soaked in whale oil and covered with dirt. Tourists in the van with me kept us at a minimum distance of about 100 yards. I used a two mega pixel camera set to automatic with a fixed zoom lens. It was set to the highest quality and I did wish for a better camera but it was at least a camera. I am surprised at the amount of people that forego bringing a camera because it isn't a pro SLR style. My opinion is that if it takes good pictures at home it'll take good pictures on vacation. It should not be a surprise to anyone that some of the best photos are due to plain luck. Being there is 80% of a picture.

Right: A large gathering of bears feed from a grey whale carcass; a large group of gulls gather on the beach

This is a shot of a male and female bears that had forced me away from their feeding area in February. About a half mile away are several whale carcasses where the game began. As it was 28 below, there was little danger of being interrupted by snowmachiners. The entire shoot lasted several hours. We started before the sun came up and it lasted until I got too cold. Even though there was time to use a tripod there wasn't the opportunity. There were nine bears when I showed up and generally I can shoot outside the vehicle when they are all busy eating. However these two had been super aggressive all week and it just wasn't a good idea to chance it. Actually I was in the process of setting up right until she came away from the other bears and he followed her.

Now standard operating procedure is to back off until the bear in question stops forcing the issue, but this girl was not to be satisfied that easily. As I said she backed me all the way off the point and into a snowdrift. The decision was to either be aggressive myself by revving the motor and moving forward, or sit tight and hope they just did the intimidation thing. I chose to sit, as bears have a memory, and once you've been intimidating they won't let

you in close again. By the way, I was intimidated. Yes I have heard all that stuff about what if they weren't bluffing and so on and so forth but then do you really want to forego a good shot just so you feel unthreatened?

Anyhow, after they backed off and started fooling around, I used a bean bag and 28 to 105mm lens with an F stop of 2.8 which is a favorite in low light. The 50mm with the F stop of 1.4 was just too big for what I was trying to accomplish. Besides once they came up to the window, then stood in front of the Hummer, I was somewhat reluctant to look away to change lenses.

Following this game my kids bought me some pepper spray so I would have a chance to shoot another day. Well, I am here to tell you they might as well throw in some oregano and garlic salt for all the good it would do. Most of us have read about the damage done by bears after a hunter has done his thing. You know what I mean, those stories of people that are buried in a pile of brush left to ripen by a bear they thought was hit hard. Think about how much damage a bear could do with only pepper spray as a deterrent. However, I believe bringing ketchup would be a little much, or at least display a defeatist attitude.

Two bears cross an ice field

In early June the sun is bright, the snow crisp and clean. That being said if you don't have a polarizing filter the results are not always, shall we say, pleasing. However in this case it worked out. I spotted the south end of this guy sticking out of a hole on the flats at Point Barrow. He was evidently feeding on some carrion he or some other bear had cached earlier. Yeah! That's right bears cache food, but then you knew that. Because and only because of the slight yellow tint of his coat I was able to spot him. Since he was on the flats and I on the ridge above him chances were if I played my cards right I shouldn't be detected. The major problem was vibration from tires rolling, so priority would be stealth mode. The plan was to place the transmission in neutral, shut down the engine and coast in as close as possible. Bears have a habit like all animals of checking surroundings periodically as they eat or nap. When this guy lifted his head he just glanced towards the south where Barrow is. Seeing how I was coming from the north it looked like a go all the way.

Remember, being detected was a real possibility at anytime, so camera had to be ready to go on a moment's notice. Because of this consideration a tripod was of no use, but the ever present bean bag was a maybe. OK, so I get in real close undetected. Now to sit and wait for him to look my way or at least get a good profile. With the engine off one gets to thinking about how long between the time he discovers the intrusion, decides fight or flight and the time it takes to start the engine and move out. My money is on the bear, but then I'll never know because the response was to ignore me. Luckily within a short time the local tour van appeared on the horizon and he sauntered across the beach and into the surf. Perhaps next time I'll find out about bear reaction time compared to mine. But then that may or may not be another story.

A bear feeding from a cache of carrion

Even though I remember the story behind each photo, I wonder, when I am gone from natural or unnatural causes, who will tell my posterity of these adventures? As I've said before, the story attached to each photo is for them, in the event they want to follow down this slippery slope perhaps they'll avoid my missteps…. Or then perhaps not. But then that might just be another story.

Anyhow, the first piece of good advice would be to avoid reading 'Alaska Bear Tales' prior to doing what I do. But in the off chance the advice comes too late, remember, the people in those stories were victims of trees, which are in short supply on the North Slope. Trees are dangerous as they keep you from seeing impending pitfalls, like hungry predators. Seeing how trees are not a consideration here it is one less excuse for becoming a victim. You can't say "he was in the thick brush behind a tree and jumped out in front of me". Nay! Nay! My friend, we'll have none of those excuses. Believe me we won't, as with no trees he is going to have you fair and square. The story told (by others) will be that you were well aware of the danger and lack of cover and got too close anyway. Which brings me to the photo here. Lying on the damp tundra is extremely uncomfortable, however, in an effort to keep my butt down and in one piece it seemed apropos at the time.

Remember in prior early fall shots I've mentioned that it is difficult to get a marketable shot because there is little texture or contrast to include? One of the ways to add color and or texture is to find some driftwood, surf or other terrain in the foreground or background. In this case I went for September grass which is brightly colored due to growing in wetland areas. All along the coast south of Barrow are large meadows dotted with ponds. If, as in this case, you walk along the bluff, you may catch a bear coming up the beach. Then the main problem is to be in position not to be seen and let the bear do what bears do. The secondary problem is to not let the bear do everything bears do. Be that as it may, my concern was focus. With grass this close to the lens and a bear in the background there is no way one can rely on auto focus. You'll notice the only thing in reasonably good focus is that one strand of grass with the seeds on the right-hand side of the photo in front of the bear's nose. This is also a free hand shot as my exit strategy did not include time to grab a tripod. Under the circumstances this is the best I could do, so it is what it is and tomorrow is another day. But then that is another story.

A bear walks through brightly colored meadowlands in Barrow

Do you remember the story of the guy walking on the beach with his grandson? Basically as they walk along the shore, a rogue wave hits and pulls his grandson out to sea. He struggles to regain his footing then goes to his knees and recounts to the Lord his history of good deeds, praying, paying tithes and such. Then he asks for one special request, to bring his grandson back. Another wave hits the beach and drops the grandson at his feet. He looks up to heaven and says "hey, he had a hat"!

Well, this bear represents that "hey, he had a hat" scenario. The Feds have been tagging bears this year as they have developed a way to radio track male bears. Prior to now only females could be radio tracked with a collar as a male's neck allowed the collar to come off. Nowadays a radio tracking device can be attached to an ear. Anyhow because of all the hassle of helicopters, tranquilizing and tagging, bears have been avoiding Barrow.

Thus getting this shot was an answer to prayers. However, now that I have time to go through the shots for the day, it comes to me that I wanted to get the guy with me to sign a release so his image can be used with the shot. Dang, as long as I was asking for favors I should have been more specific. Be that as it may I was using my favorite lens for a bear/person shot. This is the shot where a willing (gullible) companion stands outside of the vehicle with the bear behind them. Then if that willing soul co-operates, have them move back and forth until both are in focus. With a 28 to 105mm this works fairly well. Because the release wasn't obtained, what you have here is a cropped version of that photo thus losing my companion from the shot. (Cropped out, not chomped out). In my defense forgetting to get the release was partly due to this fella's silly request. He asked to have me get a shot of him in the Hummer with the bear in the background. Now how in the world did he think this shot was possible from inside the vehicle without a macro lens?

A bear runs up the beach

I respect "wet paint" signs, however the question remains "how wet? So obviously if the consensus is polar bears are dangerous, the question is "how dangerous?" With this in mind then, what would be the risk factor of taking a shot through a window? Probably not much so why not give it a go? Thus what we have here is another one of those "what if" shots. As usual thinking of what to shoot is a whole lot easier than getting the shot. An early snow got my hopes up – now to get the bears to cooperate. Realistically one can't "get" bears to do anything. You just have to have a plan that leaves room for, shall we say, adjustments. As always waiting for the moment requires discipline but good things do happen to those who wait. South of town seems to be the hot spot this year so that's where I've set up blinds.

The way currents run, there is usually quite a bit of driftwood in the area so I take advantage of this by stacking it in piles. Now what we have is a perfect place for a window to sit. All we need now is for snow to build up on the pane. Oh yeah! A bear would help. The good thing is that by leaving it here for a few days wildlife will acclimate to it, so if I sit in the blind long enough at the right time this could work out. Also I've been watching for game activity and I've pretty much got a schedule figured out.

While traveling the beaches it has become habit to watch for tracks and note the times seen. Animals are creatures of habit so if food is available they'll keep returning about the same time on basically the same line of travel. The trick is to be there before them and don't move around. Remember the vehicle is just an inanimate object. Yes I could shoot this through the Hummer window but that would then bring up a whole lot more difficulties. The main one would be how do you get snow on the window? Another concern would be "where would risk management fit in?" Actually I waited for the bear to walk by the blind knowing all the while a quick roll under the Hummer and up and in the driver's door would be no problem. My main problem has more to do with people discovering my blinds or coming by at that inopportune time. How do I get so many shots? I go out almost every day and most definitely on days with bad weather which equals no people. Originally this photo was in archives because even though I worked hard to get it, that doesn't always equate into a marketable shot. So here it is and thank you if you take it home.

A bear seen through a frosted window pane

We were sitting at the end of south pad road eating lunch. I had agreed to let this guy go with me as long as he followed my rules. Those being – don't panic, if I say freeze motion, freeze motion, if I turn and run don't ask why or look to see – just get back to the car. Oh yeah! If I say, stay in the car it's not safe, Stay!

Alright! Down the beach is a bear sniffing this, looking at that. We are waiting for her to get to where we (or I) can get out of the car without being seen and we need to have a plan. It is decided that I am getting out and he is not. Probably because I said if things got tight, dive under the vehicle and come up on the other side. The bear will most likely follow you, thus allowing time for me to get inside. The law of probability will back me up on this. Hey! I'm still alive. As life goes after awhile she got interested in some noise or activity towards the tundra. Told him roll up his window and lock the door so he doesn't accidentally fall out. (Give him some sort of feeling of safety). I slipped out and got down beside some driftwood I'd set up a few days ago.

Using a 28 to 105mm lens required somewhere closer than this. The idea is to be close in, but close enough to retreat just in case. I've often thought one of those white faux fur covers made into a suit would be cool for this sort of game. But then I might get shot by someone trying to show off a distance shot, so a coat that blends in will suffice. Anyhow, just as I'm sliding along on my belly, here comes that distraction the bear was concerned with earlier. She is now running towards the vehicle, as to her we are just another inanimate object on the beach. I calmly walk towards the vehicle at a smart pace. Crap! When I said lock the doors and roll up the windows I didn't mean mine. Briskly knocking gently on the window I request assistance. As luck would have it she changes direction and heads towards the ocean and crosses an inlet. I grabbed the camera lay down in some logs and shot over the top at that change in direction. You have a somewhat in focus shot. It was too late for a settings change from landscape to action mode but at least it wasn't a complete bust. Now about the locked door!

A bear emerges from the ocean

This photo is an August shot taken out at the old DEW line site. DEW stands for Distant Early Warning. These were high tech (at the time) radar sites linked with NORAD to detect Russian nuclear missile launches and trajectories. Currently, it's being integrated into our nation's missile defense system. Looking southwest from the landing strip is an old float plane landing area.

Most people start work about 8:30 a.m., but I start at 6:30 in order to get shots like this. Since I knew the owl was hanging out in the area it was a simple matter of getting in position and waiting for him to start hunting. I had decided the day before that I wanted a shot of him landing in the driftwood and taking off. Background is important to me and generally I prefer birds in flight to them nesting or sitting on a log or telephone pole.

When I first arrived on site he was out on the tundra hunting. Along came some research scientists who were tagging shore birds and 'eureka' he flew towards me, landing in the logs. Having waited about two hours for this, I got some real good shots of him coming in. He tucked in amongst the logs out of the wind so I just sat and waited to see what might happen. Luck was with me, as a fisherman landed his boat on the other side of the logs. This new noise caused the owl to jump up to see what made the noise. Now I would have preferred to show you a picture of when he flew away, but his wing blocked the head. All in all, I am happy with this shot, as it's better than the one I'd have got if I sat home and watched television.

A snowy owl alights on driftwood

I call this my 'Elegant Ptarmigan'. For years I've tried to get a close up of a ptarmigan, but usually they'd take off before I was within 30 feet. On this day I was shooting plastic flamingos under baleen palm trees with caribou in the background north of town. If you read bird books, they will tell you that there are no ptarmigan this far north in February, because, there isn't any feed. I discovered that on the windward side of buildings the wind hits the side of the building and blows snow off the grass. This allows birds to feed off the seeds. For your information this holds true anywhere around here where the wind is usually strong. Some of the little draws off the beach can remain relatively snow free in spots, thus, I get birds.

Anyway, the camera was set on a tripod and in order not to spook the caribou I was motionless. All of a sudden this flock of birds flies in and I am surrounded. Very slowly I turned the camera on the mount and shot in continuous mode. I didn't even check the view finder for fear of scaring them. This was a pure luck shot with the drift and the bird's breast having opposing curves. There were many pictures of the birds feeding and I did follow them once they flew off. However this is my favorite of everything I got with birds only. I say birds only as a short time later they got me in trouble with a bear. But then that's another story.

Check out the photo to the back of this collection of the bear looking at the bird in the right hand corner. Note how the color is similar. It was that kind of day.

A pltarmigan rests on the snow

Years ago October was the stormy month in Barrow. It was not unusual to have the beach road completely washed out. You can tell by the lightness of this picture fairer weather is now more common than not. At one time my advice to people was to come in October if they really wanted to see bears. With recent climate change I am now advising late November as a better bet. Now we are getting more fox, and walrus and less and less bears. As a matter of course a 70 to 210 lens is still the lens of choice as the work horse for the area. That is what was used with this picture. The 70 to 210 allows me to stay far enough away that the subject does not get stressed, yet still allows a wide range of shots. Unlike years past walrus are now finding the beach easier to rest on than the Arctic ice pack which is starting to dwindle. The good thing for me is that it makes them easier to photograph. Going out on the ice pack when it is undulating makes me nervous.

The bad thing about coming to shore is bears that have been shore bound for the warmer weather are not likely to pass up a chance at the young. Remember they haven't seen a live seal for months, so a young walrus is a tempting meal whether the mother is there or not. A female walrus can do some serious damage. A bear has to be pretty hungry to risk injury, but with a long time between meals they do try. The first day these two hit the beach it was sunny. As you can see I got some pretty good stuff. Once a walrus decides to rest in an area they have a tendency to stay for days, so I had several good sessions with this pair. That evening the photos came out dark, but I liked them anyway. However here it is two days later with snow and fog, and three hours wasted on a big male walrus and there isn't one shot that is worth printing. That seems to be the way it goes – feast or famine. By the way, even though she was on the beach and fair game for man or beast, this female ended up swimming away. I don't know whether that was because her tusks were small or she had a nursing baby. Come to think about it, the male was not bothered either.

A female walrus rests with her pup

A fox and an owl fighting

I don't want to seem one dimensional. So the last few pictures are of other animals that occupy my down time when bears are not around.

Some ask if the "Plan" is to achieve immortality through photos and stories. The answer is "No", the plan is to achieve it by not dying. However, for now we'll settle for the story.

While taking a friend to the college dormitory, I noticed several cars parked along the beach road. This usually signifies whales, walrus or bears. A bear was the drawing card. He had been on the beach but was now swimming out to sea. Knowing bear habits I figured he would go out about half a mile and when the cars left he'd come ashore in a different area. This gave me an hour to go home, change clothes and see if I could con someone into coming along as an assistant (and/or bait). Remember, if it isn't your time, not even a doctor can kill you. As luck would have it, we ended up picking the exact spot he came ashore. Photos weren't that good, but it was fun all the same. On the return trip we noticed a fox hunting lemmings amongst the hummocks. He was infringing on owl territory, so you could visualize what was going to happen. I jumped out of the vehicle and steadied the camera on the fox. As he came into the owl's area of course he had to do what any self respecting fox would do, "harass her". You know, I know, and the fox knows the owl can kick his rear end. However a fox is a fox and he'll do the same with dogs, bears or any other unwilling victim, bug them to no end. True, occasionally fox aren't as fast as they think they are or the other animal is a little quicker than they thought they were, but then that's another story. All you can do in this situation is to keep pulling the trigger and hope that it all comes out in the end. The best part, other than the actual happening, is going through all the photos at the end of the day.

I wanted to include the next two photos in this collection as it shows how ice changes so quickly. Gulls circling caught our attention. If you make a habit of watching the actions of the animals, they will tell you where to look for possible shots. We caught the bear in both these shots on separate days. The large ice formation on the left is the one that shows the most change within an overnight period. Actually there are two bears but the other one is out of our line of vision. It was quite a shock when I started to approach on foot to get the right angle. All of a sudden up pops a head and due to my extensive practice backing out of tight places away I went.

A bear plays on the ice

I got to use this back up skill two days in a row because I am slow to learn and have a habit of not seeing anything but my target. One would think I would have thought about it before, but then I never have been number one. But, you know, everyday needs a little drama otherwise they are all just Thursdays. The hope is that my 15 minutes of notoriety starts with one minute of excitement and 14 minutes of wow! Now, I liked these shots, but they didn't do as well as I thought. Maybe you can tell me what the magic formula is for getting that legendary million dollar shot. I took this one with a 28 to 105 mm lens with an F stop of 2.8. You're probably wondering about the other settings. Truth is I have no idea, as R&D for Canon took care of that when they made the sport setting.

A bear watches a pair of gulls

John Tidwell
P.O. Box 1361
Barrow, AK 99723
john@arctic-adventures.com

How about this for the first digital photographing experience of my life?

I was trying out a digital camera after using 35mm film cameras for years. Because of the expense of film and having to send it out for developing, it made sense to go digital. There was also the problem of not always getting all the rolls back from the developer. I still shoot 35mm because I am old fashioned and it's hard to give up a tried and true system. However, now, when I have film to develop, it is hand carried to the developer and picked up, not mailed anywhere. The moral to this is to know your developer, or be there when the film is processed. That being said, let's talk about the picture.

In the Arctic because of the absence of trees you can see for several miles around which can be a blessing and a curse at the same time. This bear was coming out of the east into the western sun. Since they are inquisitive expecting them to come at you in a straight line is usually not in the cards. At three or more miles it can take a bear all day or 10 minutes to get to where you've set up for a shot. You may sit for several hours and have them wander off in a different direction. Or they get 50 yards from where the set up is and they lie down and go to sleep behind some ice. Thus the blessing is the ability to see them from afar, and the curse, having to sit still until they get to where you want them to be. That, of course, is assuming they get to you at all.

True, watching a bear hunt seal, fall through soft ice, or pose on top of an iceberg is neat, but why can't they cooperate and come closer for all the good stuff? Well, my friend, this was obviously a lucky day. A dream opportunity, with a standing bear, and water dripping off her paws was like frosting on the cake. I am not going to even complain that her cubs weren't in the picture or that the sun was in the wrong spot. The ice conditions you see are typical of late May and early June with pockets of standing water along the beach. I was lying beside the left front wheel with my coat as a camera rest. Most of the time it is a good idea to sit inside the vehicle but we were on a hill above the beach and she wasn't paying us any attention. My wife was in the vehicle so I knew if the bear got out of my line of vision and started towards me she'd either scare me or the bear when she informed me of the error of my ways. A high percentage of the shots were taken as the bear first came in off the ice and of all the shots this was my favorite. On a typical trip when bears are present I can expect to take 60 or more shots and get one or two saleable. This is because most of the shots are similar so you have to throw out the duplicates. Personally I prefer landscapes with my bears but then that's what I like, not necessarily what someone else may like. We were able to get this shot because the people in my van didn't move or make noise when she looked our way. As far as she could tell the van was just another inanimate object. She never did realize we were shooting her and just kept meandering down the beach.

A bear stands in the ocean

My secret to printable pictures is the continuous shooting mode. Take as many shots as you can and hope you hit some good ones. This is one of several June bears that had been hanging around a beached whale. I had spotted the carcass earlier knowing the sun would warm the remains and help circulate the aroma which in turn attracts bears. The grease slick from an animal carcass lying partially in the water can go for miles. Bears swimming along start through this slick and zero in as if they have radar. Contrary to what most people believe, you just don't go out and get a picture every trip out 12 months a year. It is a big help having been around the Arctic for a long time and learning about the animals. Luck is probably the next biggest factor when out hunting. No matter what you know, if timing is off it just isn't going to work. November through March a respectable success rate would be 90 per cent. August through mid October is 30 per cent. April through mid-August depends solely on how much time you have to look. I got this picture by rechecking the whale several times during the day. Sometimes I see bears and still don't get a picture. The bear can be dirty, too far away; background can be ugly or some other reason.

In this case the snow bank the bear is lying on is actually on land, and the ice behind it is on the Beaufort Sea. The shot only took a 105mm lens. Anything bigger would have eliminated the background. We were able to shoot pictures until everyone ran out of film. The bear just went to sleep and ignored us. Sometimes it is so tempting to get out of the vehicle and get a better angle when they just lay around looking so sedate. Alas, discretion is the better part of valor. One of the neatest ideas for a picture that we have come up with is a bear on your shoulder. Due to this girl's lack of concern we backed off and one person at a time got out of the vehicle. Then back off a little further and get both the person and the bear in focus. What a great shot to take home! Now I wouldn't do this shot without knowing the personality of the person getting out. We've got to have an understanding that if the bear gets up for any reason, back in the vehicle you come. The safest place to do this shot is when the bear is in town or on the beach next to town. With police, wildlife, and other people to select from, what are the chances the bear will get you? Ah! Now you know another secret, it's a game of percentages in town. The easiest, most consistent place to make the shot is Point Barrow. We can set up on the ridge with the bears below and catch a shot of you photographing bears. Some settle for a picture of a bear but I like that "I was there" shot.

A bear lays in a snow bank

As you can see by the roughed up snow around this bear, she had been digging out a sleeping place for some time. This is a typical position for a female to nurse cubs, although she didn't have any with her. She had been sleeping when we first noticed her from off in the distance. As quietly as possible we inched the vehicle forward and were able to move in close enough for the shot. When I say inched I mean just that. This was an hour in the making as we were 100 yards out when we started the stalk. Once disturbed from her rest she rolled around trying to get a new position to sleep in. This is one of many photos of her, and a favorite of mine. I was using a fixed lens camera with a magnification of 4X. I suppose that is about equivalent to 105mm.

I often have people asking whether they can get a picture in close like this if they come to Barrow. That and "can I go out with you". I'll answer both those questions with some stipulations. Yes you can get a close up picture. First call ahead and see if bears have been sighted and how close. If you have the luxury of picking your time to visit it ups the percentage for success. Second questions concerned going with me. Yes, I do take people out, but unfortunately on a limited basis. I sold my tour business and only have a small vehicle to go out in. There is enough room for one other person and camera equipment. Occasionally if an extra person is small we can squeeze them in. Having sold the business I cannot compete with the old tour business on land, sea or air for awhile more. I let people ride on an availability basis at no charge. I figure so many people have purchased my pictures why not reciprocate. "What goes around comes around". Yearly I am out on vacation from last week in May through August so that makes it hard for most people, except locals, to hook up with me. What I suggest is to call the local tour companies and ask them up front about bear sightings. Typical vacation season is from May through September. If you are in this group try and make the trip in May through June. Whenever I stayed for the summer, the last two weeks of June were always good for bears, and I could get in close. I would like to give you something to think about. The Arctic is warming up, bears are losing their habitat. There is talk of getting the polar bear on the endangered species list. Now it is up to you "are you going to photograph them in the zoo or the wild"?

A bear in a dug out resting place

February and the sun is back providing great color with those clear skies. The problem is that it is the coldest month of the year. With cameras on or off, batteries bleed out real quick. To save the batteries for as long as possible, keep the camera in a case unless shooting is imminent. If not shooting, but you need it out, keep it under your coat. Store extra batteries in an inside pocket as close to your underarm as possible. I've had batteries freeze up by forgetting and placing them in a jacket pocket. When working auto focus and especially one with image stabilization lens, it is a good idea to set the camera controls to go to sleep quickly. With the window open, fingers tend to freeze. I tell people that are coming to bring gloves. Now the thinner the better is what you want, but not latex. If it were me coming to Barrow for bears, I'd invest in driving gloves something like Isotoners. I like them over other gloves as they have insulative value and you can still work camera controls. Now you kind of have an idea what circumstances this picture was shot in.

We weren't after just a shot of a bear; the idea was to make a portrait shot. The idea came from looking at a portrait of a Labrador retriever. I describe it as a "My Dog Spot" picture. Over the years pictures of bears in a hundred poses has left the problem of coming up with something different. I appreciate people coming up with suggestions or challenges of the pose they would like to see in their picture. The best chance we'd have for the portrait shot is to find a bear that would allow an approach. Either that or find a bed and sit until our victim showed up. This was a sit and wait shot. We found an area that had lots of track and sign of bears wrestling. A few beds were around so we knew it was a hot spot. Bear beds facing the sun told us that it was going to be a morning shot. We were behind a pressure ridge watching this bear hunting seals at sunup. I actually got some pretty good shots of the action but those types of shots are usually not marketable. Anyway, after having eaten its fill, it was not inclined to move too far away and found a bed. I was able to drive fairly close. This picture was taken with a 400 mm 5.6 lens on a tripod. The door to the vehicle was open, just in case the bear had any ideas concerning dessert.

A bear in the snow

A bear stands in the snow

There were remains of a seal half on the beach and half in the water. Knowing that there had been a lack of carrion on the beach, it was probably a pretty sure bet that this would bring in a bear. I had been doing a stake out here each day for a week. As nothing was happening today either, it was time to take a nap. Leaning back in the seat, placing my hat over the eyes with the sun warming up the vehicle I soon drifted off. You ever get that feeling that somebody is watching you? Well, that uneasy feeling came over me and I slowly sat up and glanced over to the right, then center, then left. Staring at the vehicle was this bear. The camera was sitting on a window mount and very slowly I reached over and it was just a matter of turning it on and shooting as many pictures as possible. There was a 210 lens on the camera and the bear wasn't really close enough to get me, but was close enough for an adrenaline rush. I liked the cold expressionless eyes and facial expression. Generally the idea is to get landscape into the photo so it can't be mistaken for something from a zoo. If it hadn't been for the tenseness of the situation I'd probably not even taken the shot. Every once in a while we all get lucky and get something good whether we deserve it or not. This is the ultimate no effort shot.

Do I remember taking each picture? Yes! Everyone has a story behind it. Consider coming to Barrow and getting your own story.

A bear plays in the ocean

These four photos are all of the same bear. It is unusual to use more than one from each session but as the water changes form so does the foreground, so I hope you enjoy my good fortune.

Photography requires a positive attitude. Like fishing, you never want to go home. If you catch something you can't stop. If you don't catch anything, you hate to leave in case something might bite. This leads me to the story concerning this photo. I was suffering withdrawal pains having not seen a bear since returning to Barrow the first week in August and here it was already the second week. Trawling for bears is a habit that is just part of my daily ritual. Wherever my vehicle is, it is noticeable because it will be the slowest one moving. It is next to impossible to notice wildlife going 60 mph. The theory is

that moving slowly increases my chances and every day I don't see a bear is one more day closer to when I will. The law of averages is one of the few that I adhere to religiously. I digress, back to the photo.

On the way to purchase building materials there were several vehicles parked alongside the beach road with occupants looking out to sea. The head of a bear in the rolling ocean got my blood pumping. Sighting this guy was only the tip of the iceberg, now to figure how to get a marketable shot, not just a shot. A decision had to be made and made fast. Once he was on shore it would be nap time. (A sleeping bear is just not that interesting). How did I know he'd go to sleep? Elementary my friend! There were no icebergs in sight therefore he had swum quite a distance and would be tired.

August beaches are basically just that, beaches. What I had to work with was one bear, water and nothing more. A landing shot or hesitation image was about all the choices available. To add to the difficulty, wave action was next to nothing. Shooting from the vehicle was not an option. Where oh where to set up for a shot? As you see lying on the beach and featuring water brings life to the image. The idea, as always, is try to ensure this won't be mistaken for something that was taken at a zoo. I am frequently asked if constantly hunting for bears gets boring. Answer is the same so far "When golf on television becomes more interesting than bear hunting; I won't be bored I'll be dead". Remember going after bears is not something you should try by yourself and sometimes is not too advisable to try with me. But come on, who wants to live forever?

We were discussing how tough it would to get a good shot on the way out to the local hardware store. September conditions were true to form, no surf, no sun. Because of the way the currents run, driftwood is rare, therefore little opportunity to include it in a photo. The thought was that an action shot or point of interest may be a substitute. That being settled the decision was to go ahead and take a look around just in case. Going out to the end of the road system was the first order of business. Scanning the beach we saw a small female heading towards Point Barrow. Chances were the male from the day before could still be hanging around. Since there was plenty of food in the area a young female may keep a big male interested in something other than his appetite, and keep them from paying too much attention to us. The game was on. As it worked out, once they noticed each other's presence it was her trying to outmaneuver him. He wanted to get chummy and she wanted nothing to do with him. We weren't even in the equation. You have both the picture of her standing up trying to see where he went and her jumping into the water to discourage him.

A bear leaps in to the ocean

Surveillance is usually boring but this was fun times. She was big on standing up and a few of those shots were acceptable. Going in and out of the water occasionally allowed some decent shots to choose from. You may notice pictures are of her and for good reason. He was way too large to move around much and covered with sand. He did give a few quick bursts of speed when she was out of sight in an attempt to head her off at the pass but she out smarted him. Three plus hours and 200 shots was a morning to remember. When dealing with more than one bear it's great to have an extra set of eyes. Luckily on this day my neighbor was good enough to hang out as back up and or possibly bait. Not really, but that didn't keep me from mentioning the possibility. Oh yeah just thought I'd mention the next day she was following him everywhere. Go figure?

A bear stands on her hind legs

I really wasn't expecting bears today. The subject was intended to be a snowy owl sitting on an antenna amongst a group of cabins. She was eyeing lemmings in the grass. Of course, my thought was, great shot if I can catch her with wings full out just as she snatched her prey. While planning the shot, I noticed three white specks in the camera lens. Thought perhaps a family of owls, better check it out. Grabbed a set of binoculars and what did I see? Three bears coming at me! Game was now on, so, bye, bye birdie, Hello bears! First order of business was to plan a shot. This requires figuring out what they are up to and where to shoot from, background / foreground that sort of thing. The other was to get Tom the manager of a local store out to see these guys. He'd come to Barrow last year and hadn't seen a polar bear yet. Anyway, figured I should get up high rather than shoot a typical level shot. By doing this I'd probably end up with a reflective view. Trouble would be to try and minimize how dirty these guys were. Also didn't want to get the typical staring off into the distance or directly at me shot. What you have here is a photo of two of the three bears coming my way prior to them swimming in the brackish water.

I did end up with a reflective view but this is another favorite from that same set of photos. I had been standing on a table on top of a hunting shack to get that reflective shot. Tom, although present, now declined to get up on the building close to me and the bears. No stopping now, so, on with the game. By this time the bears evidently had decided on a direction and were now headed for some racks of meat drying amongst these cabins. Thought was "Great" now for a head on shot. However it seemed prudent to find somewhere a tad less obvious. Was able to find a cabin unlocked so took some approach shots but then lost track of the third bear. What you have here is the last shot taken as I realized number three was missing. Felt uneasy, so exercising caution decided to step inside the cabin and bolt the door. Instincts were right as the crunch, crunch of a bear walking by the door on gravel coincided with my timely step inside and bolting the door. Saved some photos of bears among the cabins to show my wife how hard it is to focus on a bear surrounded by buildings. Camera wants to focus on near objects rather than background, therefore even with manual focus it's hard to do justice to both. Was using an 18 by 55mm lens and still couldn't quite get what I was striving for. Hope you enjoy this as much as I did taking it.

Two bears walk across gravel

Sitting at the boat ramp north of town watching a bear sleep is better than seeing no bear at all. However the bear gods were with me as I scanned the tundra behind me. The movement of a bear coming out of the water about 300 yards out caught my eye. Here was the decision, wait for this one to wake up, or go for the mover. Sleeping bears, or for that matter any bear with civilization as a backdrop, usually doesn't market well but it does, occasionally. Whereas a moving bear with a little background of nature usually does sell. The sleeping bear would be a 25 yard shot. The moving bear would be whatever. Naturally the gamble is predictable for me. I'll go for the gamble. OK! The trick would be to follow real slow and stay out of sight. This was accomplished by getting below the horizon as soon as possible. Then I made an educated guess on his progress up the beach. Before trying to get ahead and shoot the beach as a background I had to consider his habits. Most bears don't go directly anywhere but rather adopt a more look at that, sniff this, style of travel. I made a mental note of where he was compared to a mound on the beach figured in his rate of travel and took off below line of sight.

Now you might say, "hey what about engine noise?" As long as the engine isn't revving and is a steady sound the hum is simply white noise. Also remember the waves are coming in and the hill beside the bear makes the vehicle noise seem of little consequence. Another problem was how do I shoot this one safely, yet get a close up? The decision was to use a 105 lens and free hand the shot. Obviously the gamble worked and the area he'd come up at was just right on. To be honest with you this almost didn't come about. A half mile sooner I got out to check his progress and peeked over the hill above the beach then realized one more step and I would have landed on him. Luckily he didn't turn his head and look up. Got back to the vehicle alive, readjusted my nerve and ended up going further up the beach to get this shot.

A bear walks up the tundra

The grass is usually greener on the other side of the fence, but it still needs to be mowed. Evidently the choice cut of whale this small female is trying to take comes with a price. Unfortunately the price is going to be paid by the male she is facing off. The bigger bear in the background is her companion and it is a re-occurring story for these two. Several weeks have gone by with the same action, she picks a fight and he backs her up. When these two arrived a week ago this aggressive behavior began with her approaching males as they came in the area. As soon as the new bear starts showing interest, the male comes over and establishes dominance. I think she likes to give the old come on up and see me sometime line, just to get the big guy all fired up. Told the wife about what a flirt this bear was and brought her out with a video camera to get footage. We were not disappointed, as seen here she picks the fight and he backs her play. Keep in mind they are feeding on a whale so it's not as though there were no other options. I would have preferred a bright sunny day for a better photo, but then again I'd also like to go to heaven without having to die. I was using a 100 to 400mm lens on a tripod. This was one of those 80 yards out take the shot, and hope deals that kind of worked out.

Three bears fight over a whale carcass

A female bear with her triplets

What we have here are the triplets from Hollywood. Hollywood is the area that a Disney film was made years ago. We had been shooting here earlier in the day and now were back for more. Following that first shoot we had eased off the beach once the bears couldn't see us. By moving off real slow we were now able to come back and start again. When running the tour company we tried to keep bears from spooking and taking off. Even today if a bear challenges me or acts nervous I back off or leave and save them for another time. In case you are interested, I get charged on a regular basis. Always let the bear win the confrontation. Usually they settle for you backing off and giving them some space. If you were to start the engine and go out after them in an aggressive manner you win the battle, although you have lost the war, as they'll assume you are bigger and meaner and take off the next time they see you.

I still give them this respect even though I only do photography and not group tours. Also never turn the vehicle sideways if at all possible. Try and go at a bear that sees you coming, head on. If you turn sideways its bear talk for, "I am bigger than you; move out of here".

Since we knew the general area they were hanging out, it was only a short time of running alongside this floe to pick them up again. You'll notice how much open water is in the picture. As I explained earlier, about another picture, the current runs from Northeast to Southwest. What wasn't explained is that it runs fast. By fast I mean five miles an hour is common. The ice they are on is moving a lot slower than that in this shot. It is a good quarter mile long and about a hundred yards wide. Notice the open water about head high to the baby standing. This is a likely spot for a seal to pop up. When ice is blown onto the beach, it is called an evu, which is a pressure ridge that forms on land. That is one of the most impressive shows of nature's power I've ever seen. This is not stable ice where we would want to venture out. A female bear has an uncommon sensitivity to conditions and if gets dangerous she'll get her cubs out of there. Cubs that don't learn to follow mama's orders don't last long. We ended up running alongside this floe for about five miles down the beach before finding the family, so we could do this shoot. Because we had respected her earlier, we were able to hang around until some four wheelers came down to the beach. We left and they went right past the bears without seeing them.

A bear runs across the road

to purchase later. As I was slowing down, the plywood turned into a bear which promptly darted across the road. I jammed on the brakes, as hitting a bear could ruin my day. As luck would have it I slid off onto the soft shoulder. That wouldn't normally be a big deal, but my hubs for four wheel drive weren't locked in. Thank goodness luck is better than skill and the bear went back to what he was doing before I showed up, once he saw I meant no harm. There I sat weighing out the possibility of getting out and locking in the hubs before the bear figured he had my number. My luck held and some vehicles started showing up which encouraged the big guy to come back across the road and over the berm out onto the ocean.

Here is where I endanger the dog. I remembered there were large ice formations on the other side of the berm. If I could get a picture of this guy wander-

The stories attached to my photos are for my grandchildren. I want them to have an idea of what grandpa did before things went terribly wrong or I die of natural causes. I figure either way it would give them a laugh, as tragedy plus time equals comedy.

I broke my own rules on this shot. The rule is to never endanger my dog's life. If I know that it's going to be dangerous or I may do something real dumb then she stays home. You, on the other hand, are invited along. The dog has nothing to say about my adventures, while a person has a choice to go or stay. Thus if you see me out without the dog, hang around – things may get interesting. In my defense this picture was a gift totally unplanned for. I was headed out to get supplies from the local lumber yard and thought as long as there were lots of vehicles in the lot I'd check on the bear situation and perhaps have less of a line to wait in later. As I passed by the subsistence camps north of town there was a big sheet of plywood sitting next to a dumpster. I thought "great" that will be one less piece I need

ing through them or a shot of him looking back over his shoulder it might come out good. So I rolled up the windows, turned the heat up, jumped out, locked in the hubs and over the berm behind the bear I went. I figured if something happened, at least the dog would be comfortable until someone found the car. Unfortunately he kept going once he was out on the ocean and I never got much of a shot. In retrospect perhaps following him over the berm might have been a questionable decision. However, if I hadn't then I'd never know the shot I may have missed. Next time I'll try and get a bear as he turns from plywood into his true form.

A bear sniffs the air

Three bears walk down the beach

As you can see some of the ice pack has come in and these three bears are cruising the beach for whatever they can find to eat. They are actually at the furthest point north in the U.S., Point Barrow. If you were with me, and after a bear picture, this is one of the first places we'd try. Being creatures of habit, once they start hanging out in an area they have their favorite times to come in and feed, bathe or socialize. The pond they are reflected in is from snow melt. This is a prime bathing pond. I know that you've heard polar bears are not social animals but forget what you've heard; it isn't that way in Barrow. Because of the availability of food, they do tolerate and even socialize with each other when here. Mothers allow their cubs to play with other cubs as long as they are relatively the same size. I've noticed that mothers with single undersized cubs don't let this happen too often, but mothers with two cubs or a large cub don't seem as protective. A male bear is the exception. No way are males allowed around cubs.

Please keep in mind there are exceptions to every rule. As I said, this is one of the first places we'd try for a photo. What I usually do is keep a log of when and where I am seeing bears; that way someone that is only visiting for a day or so will be sure to get their bear photo. It doesn't matter how great a picture taken by someone else is, there is nothing as great as a picture you've taken with your own camera. To get your picture it's best to go out early in the morning or late in the afternoon through early morning. If you come for just a day then the best thing to do is go out the minute you get to Barrow. Most people come for the day, tour the city, and allow two hours to find a bear and get a picture before the plane leaves. Well, that works fine if there are a lot of bears in the area, but not so fine if there are not. I'll add that if you are going to go out with someone who keeps track of bears and knows the area, sometimes it doesn't matter when you go out, you'll have a really good chance to score. But if you can go out right away, your chances go way up, and you may be able to avoid having so many other people around.

Bears react negatively to pressure from too many humans. You get two or three vehicles with people making noise and trying to get in close and they'll simply go into the water and swim out to the ice. Then you end up with the same picture you always get, an animal as a small spot in your picture. What we've done getting this picture is go out as soon as the people got their luggage from the airport. They had called a day earlier and I pretty much knew that if we got out before 10 am on Tuesday there wouldn't be anyone else around and bears would still be hanging out. This proved to be the case and we simply drove out to the point and were able to set up tripods and click away. Setting up outside the van was not dangerous in this instance. With the freshwater pond as a barrier between us, everyone understood that if a bear went in the water and headed towards us, it was time to get back in the van. Generally if a bear has to cross a body of water we can shoot until it hits the half way point. The only iron clad rule is to keep the guest between me and any bear. Of course, that is only so they get a good picture.

A bear watches a ptarmigan on the ice

February is one of the coldest months of the year in the Arctic. The sun comes up around January 22 or so, and then clears skies through the first weeks of March. The cold penetrates every joint in your body. My little Suzuki has a CAT heater in the back and with the fan set on high it's barely tolerable some days. You take a 20 mile an hour wind at 30 below and you are talking serious cold. Bare skin freezes when exposed and hot water thrown into the air shatters when it hits the ground. Only people with serious mental deficiencies would be out photographing in this kind of weather.

The upside to all this misery is that in the evening we get the greatest northern lights, coupled with the brightest colors during the day. When we go out with night vision and catch polar bears and northern lights, it's one of the biggest adrenaline highs you can experience. With a full moon you don't even need the night vision, for driving or viewing. Imagine bright white snow, midnight blue shadow accents, and silver white bears lit by a huge moon. Now I'll admit that to get a bear picture to come out the way you see it under these conditions is almost impossible, but it's fun trying.

As you have probably realized this is a February picture. It was almost my last ever picture. I was out shooting pictures of plastic pink flamingos under baleen palm trees with caribou in the background. I had the camera on a tripod and a ptarmigan landed within a few feet of me. Wow! I'd never been that close to ptarmigan before so without moving my body I turned the camera and shot as many pictures as time would allow. Once they realized I wasn't an inanimate object, off they went. Proceeding up the beach I followed my quarry as they landed on the beach and out on the ice several times. I was getting carried away with the great shots so the surroundings took second place to what was being accomplished. Staying under a white tarp it was possible to get shots of tracks up the side of snowdrifts with the ptarmigan posed at the end of the trail. To make a long story short ptarmigan make quite a racket when they are all talking at once especially in the silence of the Arctic. The noise of the ptarmigan is what has wakened this bear from his nap. As you can see he is looking straight at the bird in the right corner of the picture. In all actuality he is looking at about 30 birds but they didn't fit in the frame.

The bad thing about this situation is that I am closer to him than my vehicle. Figuring my goose was cooked anyway, might as well get a picture and kids can use the money from the sale to pay funeral expenses. I continued to shoot pictures. As luck would have it, the bear looked at the birds, curled up like a dog and laid back down. If it had been a female with a cub the story more than likely wouldn't have ended this way. Cubs usually are inquisitive and probably would have spotted me and come over for a look. As a side note, the contrast of the picture was tweaked so the dark blue would be more vibrant. The dark blue comes from the reflection of the sky. Photos of the birds came out with similar contrast.

Above and right: A female bear with her two cubs

I picked up some fellow photo enthusiasts from the hotel and headed out to find bears. Before we got any further than the boat launch area north of town we found this mother and her cubs. We literally spent the whole day in this area. Unfortunately the photo enthusiasts weren't as dedicated as they thought and after a couple of hours they went to see the museum. That's why I don't do tours, photos of bears only. I never know whether the trip is going to be for an hour or all day and it is not always convenient to take people back to town. When you're on a bear it is best to stay as long as there is any chance to get a shot that may be the ONE. People can go with, and I truly enjoy the company, but I make sure they understand the game plan. True shooters never complain. They hang in until the game has run its course. Because this was a morning bear, once she finished feeding and lay down it was probably going to be a few hours before any decent shots were possible. But it was worth it as you see I've included a couple of shots of her. I actually came back with over a dozen marketable shots on this one set up.

Knowing habits really helps when out here doing my thing. It allowed going back to town for an hour to drop guests off, alert the family, then return and get all the extra photos. The plan was to go for a favorite shot, someone standing in the foreground with a bear behind them. Because she wasn't going anywhere, we have these shots for everyone that wanted one. The crowning glory of this shoot was being able to video along with stills. This is a summer land – based bear. Luckily for us she was teaching her young to fish. Every once in awhile she'd go in the water and come up with a fish. Her babies were doing the same thing. Now I don't know if the fish were already wounded or if they were active but they were wiggling when they came out of the water. Notice how healthy this family looks for October with no ice within 100 miles. She and others like her are the future of polar bears.

Some ask how I get the pictures like this when they don't see the same shot. It boils down to what I wrote earlier. When we shoot it may be an hour or all day – whatever it takes. This time out I was the last to leave – even the bear left before me. Another thing worth mentioning is that although she has two cubs, one invariably hangs close to her at all times. The other cub is the brave one and is more inquisitive. This is usual for bear families. Come to think of it humans are much the same. There is the momma's boy and then the other one that can't seem to sit still and wanders from the path, must be A.D.D. Oh yeah! We also got to watch her teach the babies how to swim under water then break through the ice and climb out on top. I believe it's time to start using video on a regular basis.

At left and right:
A female bear with her
two cubs

Here she is again, the mother with the birth mark on her nose. I've included two shots of her for this collection. If you have seen other pictures of mine then you realize she is a favorite. These were cool shots, or at least I like them. The ice field they are crossing is over a mile square and they were headed for shore. We had planned on a few hours of scanning with the hope to catch bears hunting seals. That we also got, but unfortunately animals photographed under the chance of imminent death are not a marketable commodity. Keeping in mind seeing a bear, photographing, or getting a saleable photo are all different scenarios. I had told the guys that were with me I'd show them a bear today, but couldn't say whether a good picture would be possible. We had cruised all the way to Point Barrow – then out to Plover Point before we caught her on the ice. She was moving fairly fast across the floe. I've found that with cubs so small most moms try to stay off this unstable stuff so it was a pleasant surprise to see them coming. We were on the rise above the beach and had turned the Suzuki sideways so that they could shoot through the passenger side window. I, being invincible, stood outside at the back of the Suzuki.

That is why it looks as if I am shooting from above her. I am. I walked over to the edge of the cliff, laid down for a solid camera rest and shot away. Keeping low to the horizon allowed only the top of the vehicle to be visible from the beach.

They were able to get her coming in but lost sight once she was almost on the beach. We had predetermined where she'd come to shore and had guessed right. The hope was she'd go to the right but unfortunately that was not to be. Thus another set of the south end of bears is added to the collection. Now in the old days I'd try and out flank her but I've learned to sit still and let them go where they are headed then move. By waiting we ended up catching her on a walrus further down the beach. That is what probably brought her into shore. Once they catch the smell of that oil in the water they hone in on the target from miles away.

Another good day.